SNACKS

First edition for North America published in 2014
by Barron's Educational Series, Inc.

All inquiries should be addressed to:
Barron's Educational Series, Inc.
250 Wireless Boulevard
Hauppauge, New York 11788
www.barronseduc.com

Project Director Anne McRae
Art Director Marco Nardi
Photography Brent Parker Jones
Text Edith Bailey
Editing Dale Crawford, Daphne Trotter
Food Styling Lee Blaylock
Food Preparation Mark Hockenhull
Layouts Aurora Granata

ISBN: 978-1-4380-0417-4

Library of Congress Control Number: 2013943550

Printed in China
9 8 7 6 5 4 3 2 1

 Scan and share The QR codes® in this book contain the ingredients list printed just above them. Easy and fun to use, they can be scanned by just about any smartphone or tablet, and the shopping list that pops up on your display can be forwarded and shared with a friend or partner at the supermarket, or just stored on your own device for use when shopping later in the day.

3 EASY STEPS: 1. Download onto your smartphone or tablet a "QR reader" (a simple App, often available for free); 2. Point the scanner at the QR code (the 3 black corner squares are key); 3. The shopping list pops up on your screen.

QR Codes® or Quick Response Codes are a type of barcode. They were invented in 1994 by and are a trademark of the Japanese firm Denso Wave, a subsidiary of Toyota, that granted their free use internationally. Granted patents are registered with the Patent Offices of Japan, the US, the UK and Europe.
The use of QR Codes is free of any license.
Granted QR Code patents: US 5726435 (in the USA), JP 2938338 (in Japan), EPO 0672994 (in the EU).

QR WHAT YOU EAT

SNACKS

Edith Bailey

BARRON'S

ROASTED PAPRIKA almonds

Serves
6–8
Preparation
5 min.
Cooking
8–10 min.
Level
Easy

1 large egg white

1 teaspoon smoked paprika

3 tablespoons freshly grated Parmesan cheese

2 cups (250 g) whole blanched almonds

Preheat the oven to 400°F (200°C/gas 6). Beat the egg white in a bowl with a fork until frothy.

Stir in the paprika and Parmesan. Add the almonds, stirring to coat evenly.

Spread the almonds out in a single layer in a large baking pan. Roast for 8–10 minutes, until golden.

Let cool to room temperature before serving.

4

Serve these nuts with glasses of cold beer to armchair sportsmen as they watch their favorite team play on TV.

SWEET POTATO hummus

Serves
6–8

Preparation
15 min.

Cooking
10–12 min.

Level
Easy

1 pound (500 g) sweet potatoes, peeled and cut into 1-inch (2.5-cm) cubes

1 (14-ounce/400-g) can garbanzo beans (chickpeas), drained and rinsed

¼ cup (60 ml) freshly squeezed lemon juice

¼ cup (60 ml) tahini

2 tablespoons extra-virgin olive oil

2 teaspoons ground cumin

1 clove garlic, chopped

Salt and freshly ground black pepper

Paprika, to dust

Whole-wheat (wholemeal) pita bread, to serve

Red bell pepper (capsicum), sliced, to serve

Scallions (spring onions), to serve

Put a steamer basket over a large pot filled with 2 inches (5 cm) of water and bring to a boil. Add the sweet potatoes and cook until tender, 10–12 minutes.

Transfer the sweet potatoes to a food processor. Add the garbanzo beans, lemon juice, tahini, oil, cumin, and garlic to the food processor. Chop until smooth, adding a little water if the mixture is too thick.

Season with salt and pepper and let cool to room temperature.

Spoon the hummus into a serving bowl. Dust with paprika, and serve with the pita bread, bell pepper, and scallions.

This is a healthy snack. Serve to hungry children after school or sporting events.

ORIENTAL SHRIMP bites

Serves
6–12

Preparation
20 min.

Level
Medium

1 cucumber, seeded and cut into tiny cubes

2 scallions (spring onions), finely chopped

1 fresh red chili, seeded and finely chopped

1 tablespoon coarsely chopped fresh basil leaves

1 tablespoon coarsely chopped fresh cilantro (coriander) + extra leaves, torn, to garnish

2 tablespoons coconut milk

2 tablespoons freshly squeezed lime juice

2 teaspoons Thai fish sauce

2 teaspoons superfine (caster) sugar

24 medium cooked shrimp (prawns), peeled, tails discarded, and deveined

3 tablespoons roasted peanuts, coarsely chopped

Lime wedges, to serve

Combine the cucumber, scallions, chili, basil, and cilantro in a small bowl, mixing well.

Place the coconut milk, lime juice, fish sauce, and sugar in a small bowl. Whisk to combine. Add to the cucumber mixture, stirring to combine.

Set out 24 Chinese soup spoons.

Place 2 teaspoons of cucumber mixture in each spoon. Top with a shrimp. Sprinkle with peanuts. Garnish with the extra pieces of torn cilantro. Serve with the lime wedges, to squeeze over the top.

8

These elegant little appetizers are perfect for a party spread or buffet. You will need 24 Chinese soup spoons to serve. If you don't have these spoons, you could serve them on pieces of cos lettuce leaves.

LEMON & CILANTRO hummus

Serves
8–12

Preparation
10 min.

Level
Easy

2   (14-ounce/400-g) cans garbanzo beans (chickpeas), drained and rinsed

2   cloves garlic, coarsely chopped

2   tablespoons plain, thick, Greek-style yogurt

3   tablespoons tahini

3   tablespoons extra-virgin olive oil + extra, to serve

    Finely grated zest and freshly squeezed juice of 2 unwaxed lemons

    Salt and freshly ground black pepper

½   cup coarsely chopped fresh cilantro (coriander) leaves + extra, to garnish

    Corn or tortilla chips, to serve

    Carrot sticks, to serve

Combine the garbanzo beans, garlic, yogurt, tahini, oil, and lemon zest and juice in a food processor and chop until smooth.

Season with salt and pepper. Stir in the cilantro.

Spoon the hummus into a serving bowl, drizzle with a little extra oil, and garnish with the extra cilantro. Cover and chill until ready to serve.

Serve with the corn or tortilla chips and carrot sticks.

Serve this delicious dip with pre-dinner drinks. It goes beautifully with a glass of chilled white wine.

MANGO salsa

Serves
4–6
Preparation
10 min.
Level
Easy

1   mango, peeled, pitted, and cut into small cubes (about 2 cups)

1   small red onion, finely chopped

½   cup coarsely chopped fresh cilantro (coriander) leaves

1   serrano or jalapeno chile, seeded and very finely chopped

1   tablespoon freshly squeezed lime juice

Salt and freshly ground black pepper

Tortilla chips, to serve

Combine the mango, onion, cilantro, chile, and lime juice in a bowl, mixing well. Season with salt and pepper.

Cover and chill until ready to serve.

Serve with the tortilla chips.

Serve this light and fruity salsa with plenty of tortilla chips and one of the hummus recipes on pages 6 or 10.

SEARED SCALLOPS

with sweet chili sauce

Serves
4–6

Preparation
30 min.

Cooking
50 min.

Level
Medium

Sweet Chili Sauce

1   red bell pepper (capsicum), seeded and chopped

2   fresh red chilies, seeded and chopped

½   cup (100 g) sugar

⅓   cup (90 ml) rice vinegar

⅓   cup (90 ml) water

Scallops

1   (1-inch/2.5-cm) fresh ginger, peeled

    Small bunch fresh cilantro (coriander)

2   cloves garlic, peeled

6   tablespoons (60 ml) extra-virgin olive oil

20 small to medium scallops, shucked

Sweet Chili Sauce: Combine the red bell pepper, chilies, sugar, rice vinegar, and water in a small, heavy-based pan. Bring to a boil, then simmer on low heat for 30 minutes, until the mixture turns pink.

Chop in a food processor until smooth. Return to the pan and simmer on low heat until slightly sticky, about 20 minutes.

Scallops: Combine the ginger, cilantro, and garlic in a pestle and mortar and pound to a paste.

Add 4 tablespoons of oil, mixing well. Pour over the scallops and stir until evenly coated. Thread each scallop onto a short wooden skewer.

Heat the remaining 2 tablespoons of oil in a medium frying pan until very hot. Place 4–6 skewers in the pan and cook for 2 minutes, until just golden. Turn over, and cook until golden on the other side. Set aside in a warm place while you cook the remaining skewers.

Serve the scallops warm, with the sweet chili sauce.

14

If you are pushed for time, you could serve these skewers with store-bought sweet chili sauce.

MEDITERRANEAN dip

Serves
8
Preparation
30 min.
Cooking
45–55 min.
Level
Medium

4	eggplant (aubergines)
4	red bell peppers (capsicums)
	Oil, for brushing
4	large cloves garlic, peeled
½	teaspoon ground cumin
½	teaspoon paprika
2	tablespoons freshly squeezed lemon juice
	Salt and freshly ground black pepper
1¼	cups (300 ml) plain, thick, Greek-style yogurt
	Small bunch coarsely chopped fresh cilantro (coriander)
8	pita breads, toasted, to serve

Preheat the oven to 375°F (190°C/gas 5). Lightly brush the eggplant and bell peppers with oil. Bake for 45–55 minutes, until blackened and tender.

Set the eggplant aside to cool slightly. Put the bell peppers in a plastic food bag, seal, and set aside for 15 minutes.

When the eggplant are cool enough to handle, cut in half lengthwise and use a spoon to scoop out the flesh. Place in a food processor. Discard the skins.

Halve the bell peppers. Remove the seeds and skins and add to the food processor with the eggplant. Add the garlic, cumin, paprika, and lemon juice. Season with salt and pepper. Chop until almost smooth.

Add the yogurt and cilantro and chop briefly. Spoon into a serving bowl and garnish with extra cilantro.

Serve with the pita bread.

This dip makes a delicious snack, but can also be served as an appetizer.

BLUE CHEESE & POPPY SEED crackers

Serves
6–8

Preparation
30 min. + 1 hr.
to chill

Cooking
10–15 min.

Level
Medium

1	cup (150 g) all-purpose (plain) flour
⅓	cup (90 g) cold butter, diced
¼	teaspoon mustard powder
¼	teaspoon cayenne pepper
1	tablespoon polenta
1	tablespoon black poppy seeds
1	tablespoon golden poppy seeds
	Salt
4	ounces (120 g) Gorgonzola cheese, crumbled

Combine the flour, butter, mustard powder, cayenne, polenta, both types of poppy seeds, cheese, and a pinch of salt in a bowl. Use your fingertips to rub the mixture together until a dough forms. Knead briefly until the dough comes together in a ball.

Roll the dough into a log about 10 inches (25 cm) long and 2½ inches (6 cm) in diameter. Wrap in plastic wrap (cling film) and chill for 1 hour.

Preheat the oven to 375°F (190°C/gas 5). Set out two large baking sheets.

Slice the dough into rounds about ⅓ inch (just under 1 cm) thick. Lay the crackers on the prepared baking sheets, spacing about 1 inch (2.5 cm) apart. Place a piece of cheese on each cracker.

Bake for 10–15 minutes, until just golden and the cheese is bubbling.

Leave to cool slightly before serving.

18

Gorgonzola cheese works well on these crackers, but you could also use Roquefort, Stilton, or Danish blue instead. Serve them crisp with a glass of cold white wine before dinner.

BLACK BEAN SALSA

with tortilla chips

Serves
4–6
Preparation
15 min. + 30
min. to chill
& cool
Cooking
2–4 min.
Level
Easy

1   (14-ounce/400-g) can black beans, rinsed and drained

1   medium tomato, diced

2   scallions (spring onions), finely chopped

1   jalapeno chili, seeded and finely chopped

½   cup coarsely chopped fresh cilantro (coriander)

2   tablespoons freshly squeezed lime juice

4   tablespoons (60 ml) extra-virgin olive oil

½   teaspoon coarse salt

6   large flour tortillas

Preheat an overhead broiler (grill).

Place half a cup of the black beans in a food processor and chop until coarsely ground. Transfer to a bowl. Add the remaining beans, the tomato, scallions, jalapeno, cilantro, lime juice, 2 tablespoons of oil, and salt. Stir well and chill for 30 minutes, or until ready to serve.

Cut each tortilla into eight wedges. Arrange in a single layer on a baking sheet and drizzle with the remaining 2 tablespoons of oil.

Place under the broiler and bake until crisp and golden brown, 1–2 minutes on each side.

Let the tortilla chips cool on a wire rack for 30 minutes. Serve the salsa with the chips.

This is a healthy snack that can be prepared in no time.

TOMATO & PARMESAN palmiers

Serves
6–8

Preparation
15 min. + 30 min. to chill

Cooking
10–15 min.

Level
Easy

2	(8-ounce/250-g) sheets ready-rolled puff pastry
1	cup (250 g) sun-dried tomatoes, drained and finely chopped
2	cloves garlic, finely chopped
½	cup (60 g) freshly grated Parmesan cheese
1	large egg, lightly beaten

Unroll the pastry sheets on a clean work surface.

Mix the sun-dried tomatoes, garlic, and cheese in a bowl. Spread evenly over both sheets of pastry.

With the short side facing you, take both long edges of the pastry and roll them toward each other to meet in the center. Brush some egg down the center to stick the two halves together.

Carefully lift into a baking dish and chill for 30 minutes.

Preheat the oven to 400°F (200°C/gas 6). Set out two large baking sheets.

Remove the rolls from the refrigerator and, using a sharp knife, slice into ½-inch (1-cm) thick pieces. Lay on the prepared baking sheets, cut-side up, and brush well with the remaining beaten egg.

Bake for 10–15 minutes, until puffed and golden brown.

Let cool on the baking sheets for 2–3 minutes. Transfer to a wire rack. Serve warm or at room temperature.

These are best served warm or not more than an hour or two after they come out of the oven.

FLAXSEED crackers

Serves
10–12

Preparation
20 min.

Cooking
25–30 min.

Level
Medium

½ cup (60 g) whole golden flaxseeds

1½ cups (225 g) all-purpose (plain) flour

½ teaspoon baking powder

½ teaspoon salt + extra coarse sea salt, to sprinkle

2 tablespoons butter, softened

1 tablespoon finely grated onion

1 tablespoon finely chopped fresh parsley

½ cup (120 ml) low-fat milk

1 large egg white, lightly beaten

Freshly ground black pepper

Preheat the oven to 325°F (170°C/gas 3). Set out a large baking sheet.

Grind half the flaxseeds with a pestle and mortar or in a spice grinder.

Combine the whole and ground flaxseeds, flour, baking powder, salt, and butter in a bowl and mix until the mixture resembles fine bread crumbs.

Stir in the onion and parsley. Pour in the milk and mix until the dough just comes together.

Divide the dough in half. Roll out each piece of dough on a lightly floured work surface into a 9-inch (23-cm) square.

Transfer to the baking sheet. Cut each square with a fluted pastry wheel into about 20 crackers.

Brush with the egg white and season with salt and pepper. Bake for 15 minutes, rotate the baking sheet, and continue baking for 10–15 minutes more, until the crackers are firm and golden brown.

Transfer to wire racks and let cool completely before serving.

You can nibble on these tempting little crackers any time of the day, knowing that they are not only delicious but good for you.

SPICY SHRIMP & CRAB tartlets

Serves
6
Preparation
20 min.
Cooking
20–25 min.
Level
Medium

1	(12-ounce/350-g) pack ready-rolled shortcrust pastry
2	tablespoons butter
5	scallions (spring onions), thinly sliced
1	large red chili, seeded and finely chopped
8	ounces (250 g) medium shrimp (prawns), peeled, heads and tails removed
6	ounces (180 g) canned or fresh white crab meat
	Salt and freshly ground black pepper
¾	cup (180 ml) light (single) cream
3	large egg yolks
	Bunch of fresh cilantro (coriander), coarsely chopped
	Finely grated zest of 1 unwaxed lime

Preheat the oven to 350°F (180°C/gas 4). Cut the pastry into six squares and use them to line six 4-inch (10-cm) fluted tartlet pans. Trim off the excess pastry and prick the bases with a fork.

Line each tartlet with parchment paper and fill with baking weights, dried beans, or rice. Bake for 15 minutes.

While the crusts are baking, melt the butter in a large frying pan over medium heat. Add the scallions and chili and sauté until softened, 3–4 minutes.

Add the shrimp and sauté until pink and cooked through, 2–3 minutes. Remove from the heat and stir in the crab meat. Season with salt and pepper.

Whisk the cream, egg yolks, cilantro, and lime zest in a small bowl.

Remove the paper and baking weights from the pastry cases. Spoon in the filling, then pour the egg mixture in over the top.

Bake for 15 minutes, until just set in the centers. Let stand for 10 minutes, then serve warm.

Serve these special little tarts as an appetizer or special snack. Add a mixed salad and you have an elegant light lunch for six.

SPICY CHEESE & BACON scones

Serves
8–12

Preparation
15 min.

Cooking
15–20 min.

Level
Easy

6	slices bacon, rinds removed, finely chopped
3	cups (450 g) self-rising flour
½	teaspoon salt
⅔	cup (150 g) butter, chilled and cut into cubes
2	teaspoons red pepper flakes + extra, to top
6	scallions (spring onions), finely chopped
1	cup (150 g) freshly grated mature Cheddar cheese
⅔	cup (150 ml) milk + extra, to brush

Preheat the oven to 400°F (200°C/gas 6). Dust a baking sheet with flour and set aside.

Heat a large frying pan over medium heat and dry-fry the bacon until crisp and golden, 3–5 minutes. Drain on paper towels.

Combine the flour and salt in a large bowl. Add the butter and rub it in with your fingertips until the mixture forms coarse crumbs. Stir in the red pepper flakes, scallions, bacon, and two-thirds of the cheese. Gradually add the milk and mix to make a soft dough.

Turn out onto a floured work surface and knead until the dough comes together. Press or roll out to 1 inch (2.5 cm) thick. Cut into rounds using a 2½-inch (6-cm) round cookie cutter or glass. Reroll the trimmings and make more scones. Sprinkle the tops with the remaining cheese.

Place on the prepared baking sheet. Brush lightly with the extra milk and sprinkle with the extra red pepper flakes.

Bake for 12–15 minutes, until golden brown. Transfer to a wire rack to cool. Serve warm.

These scones make a great snack any time of the day. Serve them warm, spread with a little butter for brunch, or to accompany a bowl of soup or salad for lunch.

PESTO & TOMATO *pinwheels*

Serves
8–12

Preparation
20 min. + 30
min. to freeze

Cooking
15–18 min.

Level
Easy

¼ cup (30 g) pine nuts

2 cloves garlic, chopped

1 cup (50 g) fresh basil
leaves

4 tablespoons (60 ml)
extra-virgin olive oil

Freshly ground black
pepper

¼ cup (30 g) freshly grated
Parmesan cheese

1 (14-ounce/400-g) pack
ready-rolled puff pastry

½ cup (120 g) mascarpone

½ cup (120 g) sun-dried
tomatoes, packed in olive
oil, drained and chopped

Put the pine nuts, garlic, basil, and oil in a food processor and chop until almost smooth; leave a little bit of texture in the mixture. Season with pepper and stir in the Parmesan. Set the pesto aside.

Unroll the pastry and spread evenly with the mascarpone. Top with the sun-dried tomatoes and dot evenly with the pesto. Starting from one long side, roll the pastry up into a roll. Freeze for 30 minutes.

Preheat the oven to 400°F (200°C/gas 6). Set out two large baking sheets.

Use a serrated knife to slice the pastry into 28–30 thin rounds. Place on the baking sheets, spacing well.

Bake for 15–18 minutes, until pale golden brown. Transfer to a wire rack and let cool a little.

Serve warm or at room temperature.

These pastries are best served warm. If you have any left over for the next day, reheat in the oven for 5 minutes before serving.

SPINACH muffins

Serves
10
Preparation
15 min.
Cooking
25–30 min.
Level
Easy

¾ cup (180 ml) milk

2 tablespoons butter

2 cups (100 g) baby spinach leaves

1⅔ cups (250 g) all-purpose (plain) flour

1 tablespoon baking powder

1 teaspoon baking soda (bicarbonate of soda)

½ teaspoon cayenne pepper

½ teaspoon freshly ground black pepper

½ cup (60 g) freshly grated Parmesan cheese

1 large egg, lightly beaten

8 ounces (250 g) creamy goat cheese

10 black olives

Preheat the oven to 375°F (190°C/gas 5). Lightly butter 10 cups of a standard 12-cup muffin pan.

Combine the milk and butter in a saucepan over medium and stir until the butter has melted. Stir in the spinach and bring to a boil.

Remove from the heat and pour into a food processor. Pulse until the spinach is finely chopped. Set aside to cool for 5 minutes.

Sift the flour, baking powder, and baking soda into a bowl. Season with the cayenne and black pepper. Stir in the Parmesan. Add the egg and the spinach mixture and stir with a wooden spoon until just mixed.

Spoon half the batter into the 10 prepared muffin cups. Add some of the goat cheese to each muffin cup. Top with the remaining batter. Press an olive into the top of each muffin.

Bake for 20–25 minutes, until risen and firm to the touch.

Let cool in the muffin cups for 5 minutes, then turn out onto a wire rack. Serve warm or at room temperature.

PUMPKIN & CORN muffins

Serves
6

Preparation
15 min.

Cooking
25–30 min.

Level
Easy

1½ cups (225 g) self-rising flour

½ teaspoon baking powder

6 ounces (180 g) pumpkin, peeled, seeded, coarsely grated

1 cup (120 g) canned corn (sweetcorn) kernels, drained

2 ounces (60 g) prosciutto, coarsely chopped

¼ cup (30 g) coarsely grated Parmesan cheese

2 shallots, finely chopped

2 large eggs

¾ cup (180 ml) milk

⅓ cup (90 ml) plain, thick, Greek-style yogurt

2 tablespoons pumpkin seeds

Preheat the oven to 350°F (180°C/gas 4). Lightly butter six standard muffin cups.

Sift the flour and baking powder into a bowl. Stir in the pumpkin, corn, prosciutto, Parmesan, and shallots.

Beat the eggs, milk, and yogurt in a bowl. Pour into the flour mixture and stir until just combined. Spoon the batter into the prepared pans. Sprinkle with the pumpkin seeds.

Bake for 25–30 minutes, until a toothpick inserted into the centers comes out clean.

Let cool in the muffin cups for 5 minutes, then turn out onto a wire rack. Serve warm or at room temperature.

These muffins are quick and easy to prepare and packed with healthy and energy-giving goodness.

FALAFEL

Serves
4

Preparation
15 min.

Cooking
6–8 min.

Level
Easy

1   (14-ounce/400-g) can
garbanzo beans
(chickpeas), drained
and rinsed

4   scallions (spring onions),
sliced

½   teaspoon ground cumin

2   tablespoons harissa paste

3   tablespoons freshly
squeezed lemon juice

Salt and freshly ground
black pepper

5   tablespoons (75 ml) extra-
virgin olive oil

1   cup (50 g) arugula
(rocket) leaves, to serve

Toasted pita bread, to
serve

Hummus, to serve

Put the garbanzo beans into a food processor. Add three-quarters of the scallions, the cumin, 1 tablespoon of harissa paste, and 1 tablespoon of lemon juice. Season with salt and pepper. Chop until smooth and the mixture comes together. Shape into eight small, firm falafel.

Heat 2 tablespoons of oil in a large frying pan over medium heat. Add the falafel and fry until golden, 3–4 minutes on each side.

Mix the remaining 1 tablespoon of harissa paste with the remaining 3 tablespoons of oil and remaining 2 tablespoons of lemon juice. Season with salt and pepper and add the remaining scallion.

Serve the falafel hot with the arugula, pita bread, and hummus.

Falafel originally came from Egypt, but have become a popular snack food all over the Middle East and in many other parts of the world. They can be made with garbanzo beans (chickpeas) or fava (broad) beans.

Serve them with hummus; you could try our hummus recipes on pages 6 and 10 or, if you are short on time, serve with store-bought hummus.

CHICKEN rolls

Serves
8–10

Preparation
15 min.

Cooking
20–25 min.

Level
Easy

2	boneless, skinless chicken breasts
1	clove garlic, peeled
4	slices bacon, rinds removed, chopped
4	sun-dried tomatoes, packed in oil, drained and chopped
3	tablespoons chopped fresh cilantro (coriander)
1	teaspoon ground cumin
	Salt and freshly ground black pepper
1	(14-ounce/400-g) pack ready-rolled puff pastry
1	large egg yolk, beaten
2	tablespoons sesame seeds

Preheat the oven to 400°F (200°C/gas 6). Set out a large baking sheet.

Chop the chicken and garlic in a food processor until finely ground. Add the bacon, sun-dried tomatoes, cilantro, and cumin. Season with salt and pepper and pulse briefly until well mixed.

Unroll the pastry sheet on a lightly floured work surface and cut in half lengthwise. Spread half the chicken mixture down the center of one piece of pastry, then roll up, pinching the ends together to seal. Using a sharp knife, cut into 1-inch (2.5-cm) long pieces. Repeat with the remaining piece of pastry and chicken mixture.

Place the rolls on the baking sheet, spacing evenly. Brush with the egg yolk and sprinkle with sesame seeds.

Bake for 20–25 minutes, until golden brown. Serve hot.

These rolls are a less fatty and healthier version of traditional sausage rolls. Serve them warm, or reheat just before serving.

FISH CAKES with sweet chili sauce

Serves
4–6
Preparation
30 min.
Cooking
10–15 min.
Level
Medium

Fish Cakes

4	ounces (120 g) skinless salmon fillets
4	ounces (120 g) skinless white fish fillets
6	ounces (180 g) prepared squid or cuttlefish
2	tablespoons red chili paste
4	lime leaves, shredded
12	green beans, trimmed and finely chopped
1	tablespoon Thai fish sauce
1	large egg white
1	tablespoon oyster sauce
	Peanut or vegetable oil, for deep frying
1	small cucumber, cut into small cubes, to serve
	Roasted peanuts, to serve

Chili Sauce

2	tablespoons white rice vinegar
½	cup (100 g) sugar
2	tablespoons water
5	whole red chilies

Fish Cakes: Combine the salmon, white fish, and squid in a food processor and chop until smooth. Add the chili paste and pulse until well mixed.

Combine the lime leaves, green beans, fish sauce, egg white, and oyster sauce in a bowl. Add the fish mixture and stir until smooth and well mixed. Shape the mixture into flat disks about 2 inches (5 cm) across.

Heat 1 inch (2.5 cm) of oil in a wok until very hot. Test the oil temperature by dropping in a small piece of bread; if the bread immediately turns golden and bubbles to the surface, the oil is ready. Fry the fish cakes in batches until golden brown, 3–4 minutes each batch. Scoop out with a slotted spoon and drain on paper towels.

Chili Sauce: Combine the vinegar, sugar, water, and chilies in a small saucepan. Bring to a boil, then simmer over low heat for 15 minutes. Remove from the heat.

Transfer to a food processor and blend until smooth. Strain the sauce through a fine-mesh sieve into a bowl. Scoop up 1 teaspoonful of the solids in the sieve and stir into the sauce. Discard the remaining solids.

Serve the fish cakes hot with the chilli sauce, cucumber, and peanuts.

The chili sauce will keep in the refrigerator for up to 5 days. Place in a small, screw-top jar and seal well.

SPICY CHICKEN wings

Serves
8–12

Preparation
20 min.
+ 2–12 hr. to marinate

Cooking
1 hr.

Level
Easy

3	cloves garlic, finely chopped
4	tablespoons (60 ml) extra-virgin olive oil
3	tablespoons cider vinegar
1	tablespoon paprika
1	tablespoon Worcestershire sauce
2	teaspoons celery salt
4	tablespoons sweet chili sauce
3	tablespoons honey
1	teaspoon freshly ground black pepper
3	pounds (1.5 kg) chicken wings, halved at the joint

Combine the garlic, oil, vinegar, paprika, Worcestershire sauce, celery salt, chili sauce, honey, and pepper in a large bowl.

Add the chicken wings and toss well to coat. Cover the bowl and chill in the refrigerator for at least 2 hours, or overnight.

Preheat the oven to 350°F (180°C/gas 4). Line a large baking pan with parchment paper. Drain the marinade from the chicken and reserve. Spread the wings out in the baking pan.

Bake for 30 minutes. Add the reserved marinade and toss well. Increase the oven temperature to 400°F (200°C/gas 6). Return to the oven and bake for 30 more minutes, until golden brown.

Serve warm.

These chicken wings are great food for a party. You can prepare them beforehand and pop them into the oven about an hour before you want to serve. The marinade will evaporate in the oven, leaving the chicken wings covered in a delicious sweet and sticky glaze.

STEAK fajitas

Serves
8–12

Preparation
30 min.
+ 2–12 hr. to
marinate

Cooking
10 min.

Level
Easy

2	pounds (1 kg) sirloin steak, cut into strips
5	tablespoons (75 ml) extra-virgin olive oil
4	cloves garlic, finely chopped
1	teaspoon chili powder
2	teaspoons ground coriander
1	teaspoon ground cumin
	Salt and freshly ground black pepper
16	large flour tortillas
2	red bell peppers (capsicums), seeded and cut into strips
2	yellow bell peppers (capsicums), seeded and cut into strips
12	white mushrooms, sliced
1	cup (50 g) fresh cilantro (coriander) leaves
	Sour cream, grated cheese, finely chopped red onion, tomato salsa, and guacamole, to serve

Put the steak in a glass or plastic bowl. Mix 3 tablespoons of the oil, garlic, chili powder, ground coriander, and cumin in a bowl. Season with salt and pepper.

Pour the mixture over the steak, toss well to coat, then cover and chill in the refrigerator for at least 2 hours, or overnight.

When ready to cook the meat and vegetables, wrap the tortillas in foil and place in a warm oven to heat through and soften, about 10 minutes.

Heat a large grill pan (griddle) over medium-high heat until very hot. Toss the bell peppers and mushrooms in the remaining 2 tablespoons of oil and season with salt and pepper.

Place the vegetables in the grill pan, along with the steak and its marinade. Cook, tossing often, until the vegetables and steak are cooked to your liking, 5–10 minutes.

Working quickly, spread the mixture evenly over the warmed tortillas, and top with cilantro, sour cream, grated cheese, red onion, salsa, and guacamole. Roll up the fajitas and serve hot.

A fajita is a Mexican or Tex-Mex dish made of grilled meat served on a flour or corn tortilla. Fajitas can be garnished with sour cream, grated cheese, chopped red onion, salsa, guacamole, and other flavors, as desired.

SWEDISH meatballs

Serves
8

Preparation
30 min.

Cooking
15–20 min.

Level
Easy

Meatballs

4 tablespoons (60 ml) extra-virgin olive oil

1 red onion, finely chopped

½ teaspoon dried oregano

¼ teaspoon salt

¼ teaspoon ground cumin

1 pound (500 g) ground (minced) pork

1 large egg yolk

1 tablespoon all-purpose (plain) flour + extra, to dust

1 teaspoon mustard

Freshly ground black pepper

Tomato Sauce

1 tablespoon extra-virgin olive oil

1 clove garlic, finely chopped

1 cup (250 ml) tomato passata (pressed and sieved tomatoes)

Salt and freshly ground black pepper

Coarsely grated Emmental cheese, to serve

Meatballs: Heat 2 tablespoons of the oil in a large frying pan over medium heat. Add the onion and sauté until softened, 3–4 minutes. Stir in the oregano, salt, and cumin. Remove from the heat and set aside to cool.

Put the pork in a large bowl. Add the cooked onion mixture, egg yolk, flour, and mustard. Season with pepper, then mix with your hands until well combined. Roll the mixture into small balls.

Heat the remaining 2 tablespoons of oil in the same large frying pan over medium heat. Add the meatballs and fry until evenly browned all over, about 5 minutes.

Remove the meatballs from the pan, place on a serving platter, and keep warm.

Tomato Sauce: Heat the oil in a saucepan over medium heat. Add the garlic and sauté until softened, 3–4 minutes.

Add the tomato passata, season with salt and pepper, and simmer until reduced a little, about 10 minutes.

Spoon the sauce over the meatballs and sprinkle with the grated cheese. Serve hot.

These delicious little meatballs will be a winner in any party spread. Make them small and serve with cocktail sticks for your guests to scoop them up.

CORN & ZUCCHINI FRITTERS

with guacamole

Serves
4

Preparation
15 min.

Cooking
15 min.

Level
Easy

1	cup (150 g) frozen corn (sweetcorn), thawed
1	zucchini (courgette), coarsely grated
4	scallions (spring onions), thinly sliced
3	tablespoons self-rising flour
2	large eggs, lightly beaten
2	tablespoons coarsely chopped fresh cilantro (coriander)
1	red chili, seeded and coarsely chopped
	Salt and freshly ground black pepper
4	tablespoons (60 ml) vegetable oil, for frying
	Guacamole, to serve
	Corn chips, to serve
	Lime wedges, to serve

Combine the corn in a large bowl with the zucchini, scallions, flour, eggs, cilantro, and chili. Season with salt and pepper, mixing well.

Heat the oil in a large frying pan over medium heat until very hot. Drop large tablespoons of the corn mixture into the pan and cook for 4–6 minutes, turning once, until lightly browned and cooked through. Scoop out with a slotted spoon and drain on paper towels.

Serve hot, with the guacamole, lime wedges, and corn chips.

Be sure to serve these fritters hot, straight from the pan.

SPICY CORN fritters

Serves
6-8
Preparation
20 min.
Cooking
15–20 min.
Level
Easy

¼ cup (30 g) garbanzo bean (chickpea) flour (gram flour)

¾ cup (120 g) all-purpose (plain) flour

1 cup (150 g) fine cornmeal

1 teaspoon salt

½ teaspoon baking powder

½ teaspoon turmeric powder

2 cups (300 g) frozen corn (sweetcorn) kernels, fresh or frozen

4 tablespoons (60 ml) vegetable oil

½ teaspoon cumin seeds

½ teaspoon fennel seeds

½ teaspoon mustard seeds

1 teaspoon finely chopped fresh red chili

6 scallions (spring onions), finely chopped

½ cup chopped cilantro, tender stems and leaves

1 tablespoon grated ginger

Vegetable oil, for frying

Lime wedges, to serve

Mango chutney, to serve

Combine both types of flour, the cornmeal, salt, baking powder, and turmeric in a bowl.

Chop the corn in a food processor to a coarse purée. Add the purée to flour mixture and stir well to make a stiff batter.

Heat the oil in a small pan over medium-high heat. Add cumin, fennel, and mustard seeds and cook until lightly toasted and the seeds begin to pop. Pour into the batter. Add the chili, scallions, cilantro, and ginger, and stir well.

Pour 1 inch (2.5 cm) of vegetable oil into a heavy-based, medium frying pan. Place over medium-high heat until very hot.

Using two dessert spoons, carefully drop blobs of batter into the oil. Cook until the fritters are evenly browned all over, 3–4 minutes per batch. Scoop out with a slotted spoon and drain on paper towels. Keep warm while you cook the remaining batter.

Serve hot, with wedges of lime to squeeze over the top, and mango chutney.

Serve these spicy fritters hot.

SHRIMP tempura

Serves
8–12

Preparation
15 min. + 15
min. to stand

Cooking
10–15 min.

Level
Easy

Batter

- ½ cup (75 g) cornstarch (cornflour)
- ½ cup (75 g) all-purpose (plain) flour
- 1 large egg, lightly beaten
- ¾ cup (180 ml) beer

Shrimp

- 2 cups (500 ml) vegetable oil, for deep-frying
- 1 cup (150 g) all-purpose (plain) flour
- 3 pounds (1.5 kg) uncooked large shrimp (king prawns), shelled and deveined

  Thai sweet chili sauce, to serve

Batter: Sift the cornstarch and flour into a medium bowl.

Make a well in the center and add the egg and beer and whisk until just combined. Let the batter stand for 15 minutes in a cool place.

Shrimp: Heat the oil in a deep frying pan or wok to about 365°F (185°C). If you don't have a frying thermometer, test the oil temperature by dropping a small piece of bread into the hot oil. If the bread bubbles to the surface and begins to turn golden, the oil is ready.

Place the flour on a plate and dredge the shrimp in it, coating well. Dip the shrimp into the batter, then carefully add to the hot oil. Deep-fry in batches until crisp and golden, 2–3 minutes each batch.

Scoop out with a slotted spoon and drain on paper towels. Keep warm while you cook the rest.

Serve hot, with a bowl of chili sauce for dipping.

Tempura is a Japanese word for deep-fried vegetables or seafood.

ONION BHAJIS with raita

Serves
4–6

Preparation
20 min.

Cooking
15–20 min.

Level
Medium

Bhajis

2 medium white onions

⅔ cup (100 g) garbanzo bean (chickpea) flour (gram flour)

½ teaspoon baking powder

2 teaspoons mild or hot curry powder

1 red or green chili, seeded and finely chopped

Salt

⅔ cup (150 ml) cold water

Vegetable oil, for frying

Raita

¾ cup (180 g) plain yogurt

2 tablespoons finely chopped fresh mint

1 small clove garlic, finely chopped

Salt and freshly ground black pepper

Bhajis: Finely chop one onion and thinly slice the other. Sift the flour and baking powder into a bowl. Add the curry powder, and chili, and season with salt.

Stir in the water to make a thick batter. Stir in the chopped and sliced onions until they are well coated.

Raita: Mix the yogurt, mint and garlic in a small bowl. Season with salt and pepper and chill until ready to serve.

Pour about 2 inches (5 cm) of oil into a wok or deep pan. Heat to about 365°F (185°C). If you don't have a frying thermometer, test the oil temperature by dropping a small drop of batter into the hot oil. If the batter bubbles to the surface and begins to turn golden, the oil is ready.

Add heaped tablespoons of the onion mixture to the pan, a few at a time, and fry, turning once, until evenly browned and crisp, about 3–4 minutes each batch.

Scoop out with a slotted spoon and drain on paper towels. Dust with a little salt and keep warm while you cook the remaining bhajis. Serve hot with the raita.

Bhajis are a spicy snack from India. They are usually made with onions and can be as spicy or bland as you like. Vary the amount of curry powder and chili according to what you like.

FRESH FRUIT cups

Serves
6

Preparation
20 min.

Level
Easy

1²⁄₃ cups (400 g) plain, thick Greek-style yogurt

5   tablespoons (75 ml) honey

2   teaspoons finely grated unwaxed lemon zest

1   tablespoon freshly squeezed lemon juice

1   (2-inch/5-cm) piece fresh ginger, unpeeled

1   mango, peeled, pitted, and cut into small cubes

1   cup (150 g) fresh strawberries, chopped

1   cup (150 g) fresh raspberries

¼   cup chopped fresh mint + extra leaves, to garnish

12   amaretti cookies, coarsely crumbled

Combine the yogurt, 3 tablespoons of honey, and lemon zest in a bowl and set aside.

Coarsely grate the ginger into a small bowl. Squeeze through a fine-mesh sieve or strainer placed over a bowl to get a total of 1 tablespoon of ginger juice. Discard the pulp.

Add the remaining 2 tablespoons of honey and the lemon juice to the bowl with the ginger and stir well.

Add the mango, strawberries, and raspberries and toss gently to coat.

Spoon half the fruit and juices among six large serving glasses. Spoon in the yogurt mixture and sprinkle with mint. Top with the amaretti.

Layer with the remaining fruit. Garnish with the extra mint leaves, and serve.

Vary the fruit in these cups, according to personal taste, the season, and what you have on hand.

OAT BRAN muffins

Serves
12

Preparation
30 min.

Cooking
30–40 min.

Level
Medium

2   cups (500 ml) unsweetened applesauce

½   cup (60 g) dates, pitted and chopped

1   cup (150 g) wheat bran

½   cup (120 ml) low-fat milk

1   large egg

2   tablespoons honey

¾   teaspoon finely grated fresh ginger

½   teaspoon vanilla extract (essence)

½   cup (75 g) all-purpose (plain) flour

2   tablespoons ground flaxseeds

1¼   teaspoons baking soda (bicarbonate of soda)

¼   teaspoon salt

¼   teaspoon ground allspice

¼   cup (30 g) old-fashioned rolled oats

Preheat the oven to 375°F (190°C/gas 5). Lightly grease two mini-muffin pans.

Combine the applesauce and dates in a medium saucepan over medium heat, stirring frequently, until the mixture is reduced to about 1¼ cups, 15–20 minutes.

Spread in an even layer on a rimmed baking sheet, and let cool completely.

Transfer to a large bowl, and stir in the bran, milk, egg, honey, ginger, and vanilla. Let stand for 10 minutes.

Combine the flour, flaxseeds, baking soda, salt, allspice, and oats in a bowl. Stir into the bran mixture.

Spoon the batter into prepared pans, filling to the brims.

Bake until a toothpick inserted into centers comes out clean, 15–20 minutes.

Let cool in the pans for 10 minutes. Serve warm.

These healthy, chewy muffins are great with a cup of tea or coffee.

APRICOT & NUT bars

Serves
6

Preparation
15 min. + 2–12
hr. to chill

Level
Easy

1½   cups (250 g) dried apricot
     halves

½   cup (60 g) almonds,
     toasted

2   tablespoons unsweetened
     shredded (desiccated)
     coconut, toasted

     Salt

1   ounce (30 g) dark
     chocolate, melted

Chop the apricots, almonds, 1 tablespoon of coconut, and a pinch of salt in a food processor until finely ground.

Line a 5 x 9-inch (13 x 23-cm) loaf pan with parchment paper, leaving a 2-inch (5-cm) overhang on the two long sides. Place the apricot mixture in the pan, pressing firmly to make a dense, even layer. Chill in the refrigerator for 2 hours, or overnight.

When ready to serve, use the overhanging parchment paper to remove the mixture from the pan.

Melt the chocolate in the microwave and drizzle over the bars. Sprinkle with the remaining coconut.

Slice into six bars and serve.

These tasty bars make a healthy snack. Dried apricots are packed with vitamin A and dietary fiber.

CHOCOLATE ZUCCHINI muffins

Serves
12

Preparation
15 min.

Cooking
20–25 min.

Level
Easy

½ cup (120 g) unsalted butter, melted and cooled

1 cup (200 g) sugar

1 large egg

½ teaspoon vanilla extract (essence)

1 cup (100 g) finely grated zucchini

3 tablespoons sour cream

1 cup (150 g) all-purpose (plain) flour

¼ cup (30 g) unsweetened cocoa powder

½ teaspoon salt

3½ ounces (100 g) dark chocolate, grated

12 walnut halves

Preheat the oven to 350°F (180°C/gas 4). Lightly grease a standard 12-cup muffin pan.

Beat the butter, sugar, and egg in a bowl until well combined. Stir in the vanilla, zucchini, and sour cream. Sift the flour, cocoa, and salt into a bowl, then stir into the batter. Stir in the chocolate.

Spoon the batter into the prepared pan, filling each muffin cup about two-thirds full. Press a walnut half into the top of each muffin.

Bake for 20–25 minutes, until a toothpick inserted into the centers comes out clean.

Let the muffins cool slightly in the pan on a wire rack, then turn out onto the rack and let cool completely.

Serve these muffins any time of the day, from breakfast and brunch to a late-night snack.

INDEX